Scrum and Simplification
A Manual for Cats

How the project management technique of Scrum combined with Simplification can enable you to finally make progress.

By Susan A. Anthony

Copyright © 2019 by Susan Anthony

All rights reserved.

Published in Canada and the United States.

ISBN 978-1-9995209-0-8

eBook ISBN 978-1-9995209-1-5

Jacket Image: Lucille, Maine Coon from Maine, USA wearing her University of Alberta dog jersey and hating every last second of the experience. Flick to the end of the book to see what happened next.

Photographs of Captain Murphy (grey with a white splash) and Snickers (tortoiseshell) were included with the kind permission of Morgan Tymko.

Contents

1. Introduction 6
2. Tick Tock... 10
3. Scrum... 29
4. Focus on the simple 32
5. A way forward.................................... 49
6. Where do I find simple? 73
7. Create the change you want to see..... 91
8. Leadership 110
9. Tools you can use 127
10. Changing.. 138
11. You... 153

Appendix – Scrum short guide 176

Appendix – How to estimate................... 181

Bookshelf 183

Figures

Figure 1 - Classic Waterfall 12
Figure 2 - Scrum in brief 13
Figure 3 - Sample GANTT chart 19

If you can't explain it to a six-year-old, you don't understand it yourself.

Einstein.

1. INTRODUCTION

This is a book to lead you to project and business success using the two paths of Scrum and Simplification. It's an appetiser of a book, with references at the back to books on many of the topics that this book simply summarises; like any good appetiser, sometimes that's all you need.

Scrum's name is borrowed from the sport of Rugby. A Scrum is where the opposing players gather in a huddle, bent over at the waist and locked in a tangled embrace with representatives from each team on either side of the Scrum. Each team pushes against the other to gain possession of the ball that is, essentially, on the ground.

Scrum in the project management sense is an approach to drive incremental and demonstrable progress towards a goal, typically marching through progress in two to four-week increments (known as Sprints).

Simplification and the Rules section of this book are all suggestions to position you for success with Scrum as well as just generally making things better for you at work. Why?

Time is not infinite. If we're going to spend our time on something we need to get return on our investment.

We all have endless To Do lists. Many of us have desks that look like a train wreck.

We create projects plans that we don't believe.

We each search for meaning and often come up empty.

If we could just achieve a little something each day it might help us make it through.

If we understood Scrum, we might find out that, some of the time at least, it might just help us get through the day and look forward to the next.

Scrum, like Waterfall and traditional project management and even the shoes you wear to the office is not one size fits all. Scrum can be tailored helping you deal with ambiguity. Scrum can help bring the challenge into focus and give you line of sight through its process of progressive elaboration.

When considering using Scrum, or simplifying, never judge the new by the old or you will depart depressed.

*The greatest step towards a life of simplicity
is to learn to let go.*

Steve Marboli

2. TICK TOCK

Projects are the new home for action.

Everything needs to be done yesterday.

Projects are like breathing.

We need a learn fast culture.

The projectification of everything permeates all that we do, how we speak, how we think.

When we are powerless to choose, we shrink into nothingness. If we generally assume that many of us can only really ever affect small change then we should direct our power to making changes that make life better for us and those we serve, even if they never even notice.

When we get lost in a sea of stress then no amount of willpower or wishing will help us so we need to step back and re-frame our thinking to get us out of the mud. Two things are critical to navigating stress, team-work and stress management.

Never forget though that stress is good and helps us get things done (caveman pulls hand from fire and does not get burnt) but prolonged exposure is not (modern humans get heart disease and cancers).

Work is shifting from operations and day-to-day activities into project-based work. More projects and more resources are being dedicated to projects.

The train is pulling out of the station, all aboard.

Rule # 1 – Waterfalls make you wet

First let's make sure we all understand each other. Waterfall, often known as traditional project management is when things are done one after another with no real variance in the pattern. When it's drawn as a picture, Figure 1, it looks kind of like this:

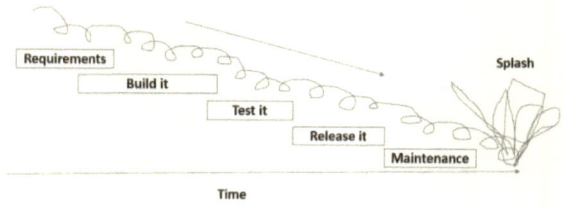

Figure 1 - Classic Waterfall

If you want to get wet and you know exactly how you want to get wet, and where, then a Waterfall is the thing for you.

If you live in a world of constant change then Waterfall, classic step by step, one foot in front of the other planning is not going to help you dance to a new beat.

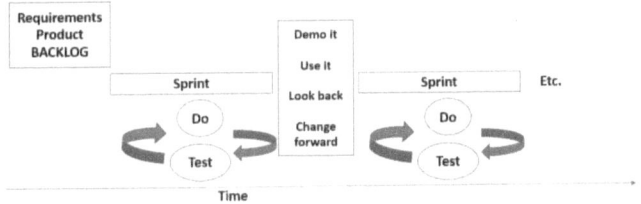

Figure 2 - Scrum in brief

Scrum, depicted in Figure 2, has the following major components:

1. **The Product Backlog** This is the list of your requirements for what you want to do plus an estimate for the time to complete each item. The duration for each item needs to be less than the length of a sprint so you need to chunk big pieces of work accordingly.
2. **Sprints** are a period of time when work items from the Product Backlog are chosen to be worked on. This decision is done in conjunction with the Product Owner (the Sponsor).

3. **Daily Stand-ups** (yes, that means you don't sit down), typically fifteen minutes in duration, where the team answers three important questions:
    - What did you do since the last Stand-up?
    - What do you plan to do before the next Stand-up?
    - What obstacles are blocking your progress?

Rule # 2 - Stress management

On any given day we can each draw up a big list of stressors but some are more destructive than others. Bosses that are very strict and that allow no freedom to do the job cause stress. Sometimes the only way through that is to be fully submissive ... kind of demeaning but sometimes survival is the strategy while we plot our escape. Good bosses encourage you to think. They take new approaches and use phrases like, 'we don't have problems, we just have decisions.'

Boss anxiety can cause a lot of dissatisfaction, no-one volunteers, worried that if they fail, they'll never get back into the promotion pack.

There is no easy (legal) solution for a stress-inducing boss but you can work to minimise your stress in other ways (including sitting in your

favourite bag as Captain Murphy is demonstrating).

Simple tips for overall stress management are to feel a sense of achievement every day:

- Find something you can finish each day, however small.

- Give your full concentration to it and be present for it and the people involved.

Achieving, and then remembering those achievements, can get your through the day, ready for the next.

Rule # 3 - Beauty is only skin deep

Beautiful plans. Beautiful charts. Fabulous Gantt charts, what are they again? Figure 3 is a simple example of a Gantt chart. The length of time to complete the project is the sum of the time it takes to complete each of the longest duration tasks together. This path through a project is known as the Critical Path.

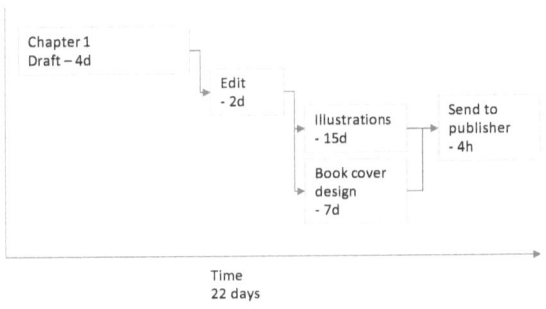

Figure 3 - Sample GANTT chart

The world is a grimy place and people can't even wait for twenty two days for a chapter to complete without changing their mind.

Scrum considers how people actually work not their desired, some might even say, fantasy of how work might be if they wished hard enough. It's a messy process racing through a Sprint, getting to a good enough state but in an environment of change it is far more realistic.

Rule # 4 – Flow with it

Flow can't be described but it can be felt. It's when time passes and you barely notice. Not when you are binge watching TV shows but when you are working. Something has your attention and you are making progress. Impediments are removed before they become impediments, like sweeping the ice in Curling or blocking in Football or catching a child before they fall and they shout at you for spoiling their game.

Recently, I made a cake. Not just any cake, a Victoria Sandwich. This is a classic cake and requires time to make. I've been making this cake since I was eleven years' old, even taught other people how to make it. Recently though the cake has been horrible. I blamed living at altitude but the real issue was my lack of focus and corner cutting. The most recent time I made it I focussed entirely on it and finally I understood something that I had nodded to but never fully got, flow.

I learnt about flow watching a National Geographic film and one of the features was about an elderly woman on the Isle of Harris (off the west coast of Scotland – bleak, barren and beautiful), a weaver of something called Harris tweed. This interested me because weaving is both fascinating and fraught with danger, lose attention and the cloth is ruined. When asked how she produced such magnificent cloth she replied, "When I weave, I weave.". That day when I pushed all things from my mind and baked my cake I too could say, "When I bake, I bake." I was in the zone and it felt good and the results showed it.

Flushed with success I turned my attention to socks. 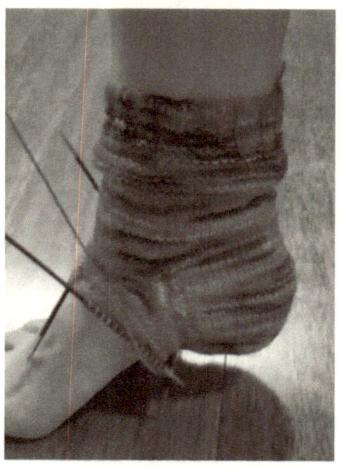 The challenge with complexity and multi-tasking is that we only scratch the surface of the zone. A goal of simplification is to strip away the unnecessary to give us the opportunity to take what was once wool and is now the heel of a sock!

Rule # 5 – Ignore generational factors

I could take a few pages to explain to you why Traditionalists will defer to authority and that when the authority figure says 'Do it!' they say 'How high?' on the way up and that Gen Xers want to be individuals etcetera (yes, that's what etc. looks like without the .) but this would obscure simplification. I believe all generations need to consider that if we want to:

- Do a better job
- Work hard
- Achieve success

Then we all need to simplify. Period.

Rule # 6 – Do NOT create a Simplification or Scrum project

Many of us love initiatives, some love to hate them, but they do break up the day. In the case of Simplification or starting to use Scrum, the reality is that if you create a 'Simplification project' or a 'Scrum trial' then you create two opportunities and they are:

1. The ability to put it on a board with other work and watch it be debated and cancelled.
2. Or see it de-prioritized, pushed to the bottom of the pile.

Simplification is like breathing and should be treated accordingly as ESSENTIAL just like Payroll is to employees and servers staying up are to IT.

The other way to make the project open to cancellation or re-prioritization is to make it an Organisational Development (OD) project. For some leaders even a whiff of OD can feel like a dose of psychotherapy and they may consciously or subconsciously sabotage it. The best OD efforts are always those that stalk you like game in the woods and gobble you up before you blink. Great examples would be having optional, free Scrum training with supportive emails explaining how it helped this team and that team. Nudge them to it, no lash required.

Build it and they will come…

*Any darn fool can make something complex;
it takes a genius to make something simple.*

Pete Seeger.

3. SCRUM

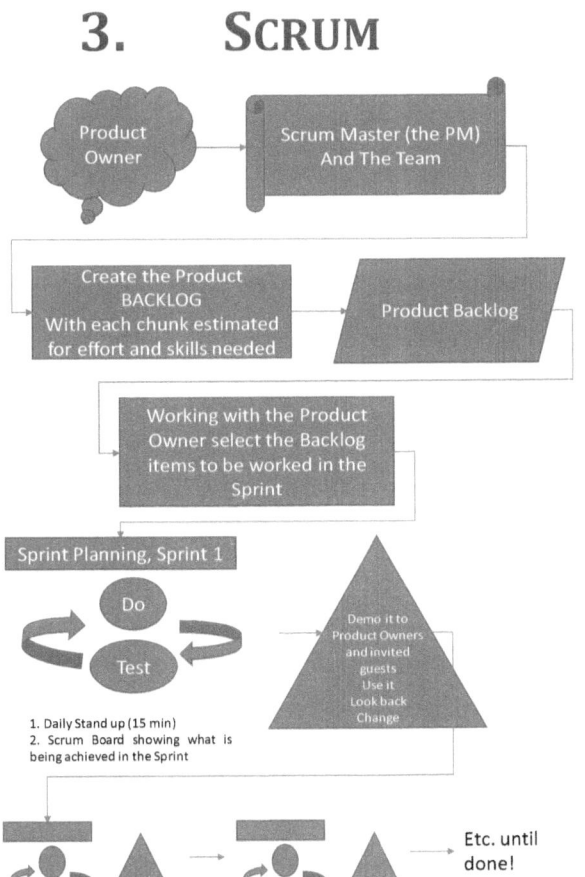

The PRODUCT OWNER needs to be that singular kind of person who is committed. They will help remove obstacles. They will work closely with the Scrum Master.

The SCRUM MASTER is best thought of as a Project Manager. Many are certified for this role but some IMAGINE SUCCESS and succeed.

Every item on the PRODUCT BACKLOG needs to be estimated – refer to the appendix.

SPRINTS are just period of time when the agreed list of items from the Product Backlog are worked on, typically two weeks. The SPRINT PLAN is developed with the Product Owner for each Sprint to ensure priority items are worked first.

Scrum works well if progress is visible. The SCRUM BOARD shows TO DO, DOING,

DONE for each SPRINT and overall for the project.

These are just the basics, check out the Bookshelf for more detail.

4. FOCUS ON THE SIMPLE

Simple never means easy. Neither does it mean not complex. It means not tangled up like wool in a kitten's paws. Not convoluted.

Scrum may seem quite obvious to anyone who has avoided project work or perhaps has just been born. To do. Doing. Done. You have to admit, it's easy to remember.

Scrum is about demonstrating and delivering progress towards goals:

- Not a silver bullet.
- Helps you to Fail Fast.
- Deliver progress every two to four weeks.

- Makes sharing knowledge the expected approach and the new normal.
- Encourage you to ask for help.

However, before you start you really need to understand what you want to achieve. The following quote is bigger than the average project but you cannot beat it for laying out the goal:

First, I believe that this nation should commit itself to achieving the goal, before this decade is out, of landing a man on the moon and returning him safely to the Earth

John F. Kennedy, May 25, 1961

Rule # 7 - Learn about simplifying from the Japanese

I have nothing against the tidying challenged. Over my career I have seen all kinds of behaviour from those who had their own clear desk policy, whose room was basically immaculate, to someone who perhaps might have been considered a hoarder with a mild clinical condition. Personally, I am more 'clean desk' but not entirely. However, here's what Marie Kondo taught me from her part biography, part self-help book:

- People cannot change their habits without first changing their way of thinking.

- It's not worth bothering, I was born this way/it is the way it is … wrong!
- Visualize where you want to get to – in the case of tidying, a clutter-free space.
- Quietly work on your own area first as a model to those around you.
- Don't bother over-categorising, make broad groupings since searching them will take as much time as sorting through your own folders (systems that generally only make sense to you).
- Look for methods that tell you at a glance what the status of something is, for example, a box of forms should be open at one edge so you can see how many are left. A lid would create an

extra step and the extra sides mean you have to look inside. Give yourself clues.

- Vertical storage – Kondo suggests rolling up things like t-shirts and standing them on their edge so when you look in the drawer you can see them all and better choose. This advice is quite brilliant and has allowed many of my old T-shirts to see the light of day. What visual clues could be used in your work? Tires on their side, easy to count. Bandages, sideways?
- "When we really delve into the reasons why we can't let something go, there are only two (reasons): an attachment to the past (the way it was) or a fear for the future."

Rule # 8 – Eliminate Administrative Clutter

Ask yourself:

- Are we doing the right things?
- Are we doing the right things right?
- Are we doing enough of the right things?

By all means check work but check with a purpose and a corrective action plan.

Rule # 9 – Simplify your message

Remember your retirement.

Take 30 minutes of exercise every day, keep Dementia away.

No-one remembers complex messages. People, it seems, can hardly follow simple messages like cigarettes can damage your health so is it any wonder that Climate Change remains a mystery to many. A great example is the wellness story. As we are bombarded with messages that conflict eventually you reach the *past caring* point and we go back to deep fried chocolate bars (if you're interested, they dip them in batter first otherwise there is an unholy mess in the fryer).

Simpler messages can be starker, the one illustrated is a nod to the benefits of daily exercise to stave off dementia. The poster hints at cycling in a beautiful place and tries to get you to visualise the merits of exercise as a way to keep dementia, the fear of all boomers, at bay.

Rule # 10 - Don't measure the wrong things

Scrum projects measure progress every day and wrap-up that progress every two to four weeks depending on the duration you agreed for your Sprint. Sprint measures are such things as how many tasks you complete each Sprint. This helps you decide how much you can achieve in the next Sprint and in time help you forecast an end date.

A classic mistake in measuring is Over-fitting, where the work is shaped to the metric (rather than the other way around). This creates bad metrics as in this example: Number of calls to the Help center less than ten could result in no-one picking up the phone after the ninth call. Hardly the result the lonely user is looking for.

Compensation is also a classic case of over-fitting where bonus targets can focus us on the wrong problem and guarantee overall failure.

Think carefully before you measure.

Rule # 11 - Don't take more than you really need

Taking more than you need can badly impact those new to Scrum who think they should pile everything, almost, into the first Sprint. Surprise! Fail! Or people tag themselves against too many tasks.

The 'Tragedy of the Commons' is where we each take a little more than we need.

In the case of the Tragedy of the Commons people let their sheep graze on common land until there was none. Something similar is happening with over-fishing and the forced extinction of butterflies collected by people in far-away lands.

This is what we do to the people who work in unnecessarily complex environments, we rob them of the ability to succeed and we remove their ability to succeed at even one small thing each day until they burst and die in their job.

Rule # 12 – Choose to simplify

Companies with deep pockets, or governments who have the luxury of ours, are fond of consulting, this is intended to create a feeling of inclusion. The reality is that the 'consultation' is really 'inform' because they are not truly seeking your feedback, they are trying to get you to self-soothe like a baby and then they will move on with their plan.

Simplification is perhaps the only real choice a person can get away with and even then, there will be a layer where even that ability will stop.

When you simplify something don't forget:

- Ask for, or appreciate, crisp and immediate feedback.

- Adjust what you are doing, you won't regret it.

Scrum is all about feedback, constant and unrelenting. It will not suit everyone but if you can bend to its needs then you will be happy with the results.

Don't worry if you fail at first, this can happen in small teams where someone resists and it becomes too hard. Look instead to Scrum by stealth, manage the To Do, Doing, Done yourself and hand out tasks.

Rule # 13 - Realise that ASAP takes longer than you think

Even, or perhaps, especially in Scrum worlds you may still hear, ASAP – As Soon As Possible.

Did you know that it is generally quicker to specify a deadline than say ASAP since ASAP is no time at all and it's only a person's perverse logic, actually, I'll go further, their laziness, of not wanting to prioritize this new task against others they have likely thrust upon you that makes them say ASAP. Always, always, ask for a date and hold your ground while you prioritize the item with them against their other requests. If this results in hysteria refer to the earlier section on how to kill your boss and make it look like an accident (might be an Appendix).

When my husband worked for a semi-conductor company that will rename nameless it was often said that there was always time to do it twice but never time to do it right the first time. It's not their adage but it applied very well and it can apply to many companies.

You should avoid complicatedness and be ruthless and uncompromising in dealing with it, because complicatedness paralyzes an organisation and make you unproductive.

Simon Riis-Hansem

Senior Vice President, Executive HR, The LEGO group

5. A WAY FORWARD

Create the right environment:

- Co-locate the team. This allows quick communication and if it's a small team with more than one project you will get to experience their challenges and can be more appreciative of shared resources. Of course, ideally there are no shared resources...ha ha.
- Short daily meetings. The Daily Stand-up needs to stay within fifteen minutes. Some people, myself included, can't always stay on topic. This is where a visual Scrum Board works best.

- Eliminate/reduce multi-tasking. We are a single machine, we can't do two things at once. I cannot concentrate on a chick flick and figure out what my husband is saying in the background. Because it's thinking we believe it's possible, it isn't. Imagine fixing a car and baking a cake…at the same time.

Your Project's Requirement List = Product Backlog.

Step 1:

Take the project's requirements list:

a. Create a list of all the work that needs to be done and split it into chunks.
b. Each chunk needs to have a tangible deliverable (e.g. a list of data, a working

screen, a user handout, a form, a set of interviews).
c. For each chunk, who needs to help?
d. Is that chunk of work: Small (few hours), Medium (maybe a day) or Large (a few days – and if so, can it be split into smaller chunks?)?
e. Sort the list into priority order with the most important items at the top. You will need to consider chunks that are needed first before another chunk can be worked on, for example, interview questions prepared *before* the interviews. You now have your Product Backlog.

Step 2:

a. What can be done by the next meeting (the Sprint Review)?

Step 3:

Using a whiteboard, noticeboard, spare piece of wall, any large surface devoid of artwork, create your own tracking system with sticky notes of all the chunks of project work you are doing for this Sprint. Start them all in the To Do column and move them over as you complete them:

All the project chunks	To Do for this Sprint	Doing	Done
...	...	...	...

This is known as a Kanban board.

Step 4:

Meet every single business day for a Stand-up (as in standing only) for no more than 15 minutes ideally at a set time each day. Each person answers the following questions:

a. What was done yesterday to finish the Sprint?

b. What will be done today?
c. What are the obstacles to achieving the goal?

Step 5:

The Sprint Review becomes:

a. What was accomplished since the last Review with an actual artefact like a process or a job description or something you can proudly show people.
b. Is that item completely ready to go, no more work (on that chunk not the total project)?

At the meeting you then ask – in a blame-free way:

a. What went right?
b. What could have been better? What would make you happier?
c. What one improvement can we make to help work be better in the next Sprint?

Rinse and repeat until done.

Now can we go for a walk?

Rule # 14 – Check. Check. Check.

The essence of Scrum is checking, and checking, and checking again that what is being done is still what is wanted until there it is, as if by magic.

This magic is achieved by showing and discussing progress with the Product Owner (known as a Sponsor in classic project management), continuously.

Checking is achieved when:

- Discussing and agreeing what you are going to do (the Product Backlog).

- Planning what from the Product Backlog goes into each Sprint

- Reviewing at the end of the Sprint

The Product Owner collaborates with the team every step, helping remove obstacles to progress.

During the Daily Stand-Ups the Scrum Master (similar role to the Project Manager) is directing the team, managing progress. The Product Owner does not, generally, attend these daily meetings.

Phase Gate processes check too (you know those giant meetings where everyone spends weeks pulling the slides together and then the review is compressed into the last fifteen minutes and an executive finally snaps and kills the project or pushes for some crazy date). But do they really check? Did I say that out loud? A Product Owner in lockstep with the team is a more powerful resource than a team of distant strangers (although Red Teaming is an area where strangers can drive us to do the right thing through constructive feedback).

Rule # 15 – Question less if you crave bliss

Considering religious indoctrination (in Lyengar's research with Seligman) but applying it to a business hierarchy, those who accept the god-like nature of their superior may be more likely to acquiesce to their rules (believe in god as per Lyengar). Those that question more are more likely to experience the feeling of being trapped (not believe in god).

It's important to know who you are and behave accordingly, you will be happier and reach bliss sooner. Question more, and you'll likely be picked to lead a Red Team and question, in a devil's advocate kind of way, pretty much anything.

I fall on the side of the latter and so perhaps am less likely to be in bliss anytime soon. Victor Frankl understood that the real search is not for bliss but for meaning. I get my meaning through achieving and Scrum and Simplification help that journey.

Rule # 16 – Control your life, a little

The Whitehall Study started in 1967 and ran for over a decade under Professor Michael Marmot of University College London. The study taught us that lack of control over your life, lack of opportunity to participate socially in a meaningful way, could affect whole societies, not just people. In the case of his study the area of particular concern was how lack of control drove up the incidents of cardiovascular disease.

This builds on my own favourite Stress book, if only for the title, Why Zebras Don't Get Ulcers, by Robert M. Sapolsky where, amongst a wealth of material, he suggests that when attempting to exercise control, don't try to control what has already happened, seek control in the present moment. Don't even try and control the future, find what he calls, 'footholds of control, each one small but still capable of giving support, that will allow you to scale the wall.'

He also urges finding an outlet for your frustrations and doing that outlet often!

In the face of strong winds, let me be a blade of grass.

In the face of strong walls, let me be a gale of wind.

(Source: Quakers)

Choose your battles, your strong walls, carefully and then give it all you've got.

What Sheena Lyengar calls the 'Call of the Wild' is a proven desire to make choices, however small, as a way to enjoy life. She tells us not to choose a plant for the resident of a retirement home. Let them choose it. Let them choose to water it. These are the steps that will improve life for them. Exercise choice, you will feel all the better for it.

If all else fails and you really have no control over your office life and knowing that having low control of your life is a predictor of ill-health then:

>Choose a plant for your office.

>Water it.

OR

>Choose an ornament for your desk.

>Decorate it.

OR

>Seek another profession or job.

Rule # 17 - Get it into one page or one idea or one place

Edward R. Tufte's books show us a myriad of ways to express data better so that it becomes information. Information that is easily absorbed and adds to our understanding rather than obscuring the underlying meaning.

It will take longer to make it one page but the time spent by you will save a lot of time for others.

First, though figure out what you want to say, write it, then edit the heck out of it. If you can turn it into one picture then so much the better. Check out Chapter 3 for inspiration.

Rule # 18 - Make decisions quickly

If you are overloaded or bored by all the detail then likely you are involved in too many decisions. You may not be able to make every decision quickly but if not, like email that you have scanned and sort of read but left unfiled, you will keep coming back to them and you will waste more time than your procrastination saved.

Remember, we are trying to move promptly through the Scrum Sprint to get things done!

Could you be a control freak?

There are worse things than making a decision and moving on.

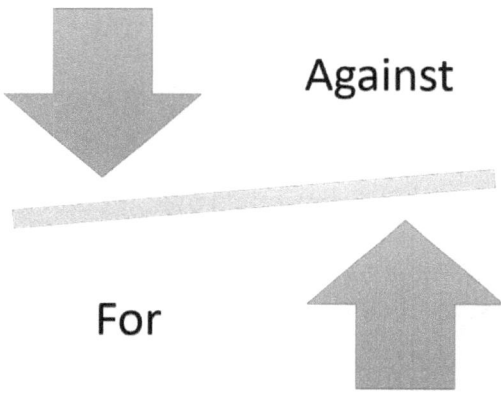

Rule # 19 - Give yourself tight timelines

It's harsh but combined with reduced multi-tasking, giving yourself tight timelines, like the Sprint (one, two or four weeks), will create laser focus, as Lucille is demonstrating.

There will always be more you could have done but eventually you need to fish, cut bait or peel the train right off the tracks.

Is what you are doing in the Sprint enough for now? Enough to get it up and running? Then, you are done. Save refinements for the future. Keep moving.

Rule # 20 - Build on success

Think like nature. Think like Evolution. Mother Nature has taken a million wrong turns and hit millions of dead ends. She has the benefit of millenniums, you only have millennials and the rest of the generationals.

Take a change that helps, discard or mask one that doesn't.

Learn from what didn't work, it might work in the future but for now, shelve it.

Move on.

Rule # 21 - Sensemaking

Help yourself and your team if applicable make sense of what you are doing.

Think like a jigsaw puzzle. Work the edges, work a cloud, but keep working.

At first, it's maybe just the big things but overtime you fill in the details. You are looking for plausible versus one hundred percent accurate.

6. Where do I find simple?

The books about Scrum are long. The training is intense. Certificates are handed out. There is a fair amount involved in doing it well. Apply Scrum techniques to learning about Scrum, treat this book as the first Sprint.

I'm confident it is hard but just like project management most people are going to just try it for themselves, certification be damned.

The books about Project Management are numerous. The training is intense. Masters degrees are handed out, I have one!

Sometimes you need to try something, and maybe not get it perfect but at least give it go. I believe that Scrum is just such a technique. You can learn enough to try it and if you like it then you can move up to books, refer to the Bookshelf, dedicated to the topic.

The key to thinking Scrum is thinking Simple. This chapter talks about examples of simplification to get your mind to overcome any bias you may have about it being too easy. It's not easy. It's hard. Hard like standing on the harbour wall with waves lashing you and wind buffeting you and you determined to stay there and take it. That kind of hard.

Complex? That's easy...but:

If we overvalue simplicity, we might get distracted and end up overcorrecting, cutting to the bone and reducing complexity long after such reductions cease to be wise or productive. Course corrections are important, but we must be careful not to lose sight of the objective.

Dan Ward, The Simplicity Cycle, 2015

Rule # 22 - Simple machines

If you're not an engineer, or that way inclined, you may not know that there are six basic machines:

1. LEVER …use a screwdriver to open the lid of a paint can
2. WHEEL and AXLE …your bike
3. INCLINED PLANE …playground slide
4. WEDGE…axe to split a log
5. PULLEY…opening your window blinds
6. SCREW…your faucet

Each of these small parts, builds up, compounds, to create cars, elevators, trains, so it is with each Sprint.

Rule # 23 - Bureaucracy applications

The humble form is what most of us would think of when we think of bureaucratic systems. Forms can bring us to our knees. Forms that require a signature suffocate us like snow in an avalanche.

Designing a good one is very hard. Creating as few as possible is almost impossible. Making the transmission of the form convenient frequently fails to cross anyone's mind. It doesn't work for everything but once discovered you will wonder how you ever lived without them. If you've never heard of them then Microsoft Help or 'the Google' will help.

- Use email templates (Microsoft Outlook).
- Store the templates with your signatures.
- Make that the last signature they see.

If I'm sending the template to you and you send it back, other than life insurance that frequently seems wedded to physical signatures, that's all the 'signature' you need. Isn't it?

Rule # 24 - Where to start

When you are building your Scrum Backlog sometimes you may need to step back and determine what you need to do. A good tool for this purpose is the Force-field analysis. Works alone or in groups.

Take an area of complexity and consider this worked example:

- Desired goal
    - Universally completed beneficiary form to show who will receive insurance benefits in the event of death
- Current situation
    - Beneficiaries not specified
    - Monies go to the estate and take a long time to reach loved ones,

or not, depending on any legal challenges
- Lot of back and forth with relatives to explain what is going on. Waste of employee time and not a good use of loved ones' time. Can lead to frustration and dissatisfaction.
- Why do we want to simplify (give them a score out of 5 where 5 is strong)?
  - Lot of errors…4/5
  - Lot of questions that the item is supposed to answer…4/5
  - Lack of enrolment…3/5
- Then consider what is the restraint
  - The date field isn't explained so the date is entered incorrectly
  - Don't understand why they have to specify a beneficiary
  - Don't bother because the process steps are long and complex

- For each restraint agree a next step and who will complete that next step
- Agree a point in time to come back and discuss progress. This can also work well for individuals planning their work, we all need targets.

Rule # 25 – Remember, People don't read

Shocking but people don't read and they especially don't read signs or instructions, as one hospital visitor told me as she attempted to barge into the hospital room my husband was sleeping in. Pushing through the closed glass door that had a sign stating NO ENTRY after a certain time; it was after that time.

"Oh, I don't read signs."

To which I replied, "Well let me abbreviate it for you, Get Out."

Knowing people don't read, it's pointless to put anything important in the middle or likely at the end of anything. You need to get the so-called elevator pitch smack in their face. Consider this approach to emails for the reading challenged especially to your Project Owner:

Title: <What I want you to do>

<My summary message>

<My laborious detail>

<My summary again assuming you made it this far>

Of course, you can use this against them by hiding a confession somewhere in the middle. Eighteen years of religious education taught me to bury the big sin and follow it up with something trivial but distracting, or a question, either works.

Rule # 26 -
Laugh...a lot

Simplification can result in job loss. This can be scary. Create humour around situations and people will tolerate them better, it's not called 'gallows humour' for nothing (gallows are where they used to execute people by hanging them by the neck – at some point in the future no-one will be able to fathom that anyone could do this and I hope I live long enough to have to explain this, like candles pre-electricity. Yes, candles were once used to deliver things other than scent.).

Use storytelling and entertain – you don't have to be a stand-up comic but bringing out the funny side will be a lot more memorable than the horror of it all. Gruesome tales should be especially avoided at bed-time as they solidify overnight into disturbing memories. Did you know? It is now felt good process not to go to bed after something traumatic and allow your waking brain to process what happened before your sleeping brain gets a hold of it and does lord knows what to the memory and drives you closer to PTSD.

Important safety tip: If no-one is laughing…move on…quickly.

Rule # 27 - Use PowerPoint wisely

Bullets, bullets, and more bullets. Who hasn't hated the phrase, "get me a few slides on that, and we'll talk" followed by "send it to <person x> too so they can weigh in"? Then you end up with the issue so summarized it fails to make sense and absolutely not to person X who wasn't involved in the initial discussion. However, if you can coherently distil it into a PowerPoint slide, or slides, then that is a rare gift.

Whilst it is important to make decisions quickly it doesn't mean there can't be some lead up and preparation. How nice to receive material in advance to consider and react to when the discussion comes so that the 'quick decision' is actually a reasoned decision and not just to make it go away.

OK, you can use PowerPoint to summarise your points but make it simple! And, use it with intention.

Rule # 28 - Do what you can?

We have all worked in headless chicken mode, feathered corpses littering offices and public transportation every day. We can't always change that so here are some coping techniques:

- Choose 3 important tasks to complete each day (or just the one thing if it's that bad)
- Turn off your email … try for a full hour without interruptions. If you have a door, use it.
- Book 20 minutes a week to step back and plan your time. Make it a private meeting.

Always ask, "Is it worth my time?"

Important note: If your boss thinks it's worth your time, then it's worth your time. In this scenario, master the art of grovelling apology for all those you will now let down if your negotiations fail to place your Boss's needs below that of others. And also remember, that there will be at least one person who will make you pay for that apology by attempting to demean you publicly later. There is a special place in hell for that type of colleague and we'll leave it at that.

Simplification is often about the small and not the large and not the podium winner.

If you seek praise you are in the wrong line of work.

All of you have had mistakes and failures ...the question is, what would you do differently this time?

John Chambers

Speaking with the New York Times
August 2009

7. CREATE THE CHANGE YOU WANT TO SEE

Maybe you don't run an entire project or a big project, maybe it's just about you.

Maybe all you can do is a better job of managing your mammoth To Do list. What could that look like?

You eat an elephant, one bite at a time.

Applying the Time Management adage of 'eat an elephant one bite at a time' you can manage your own TO DO list in a way that helps you see what's going on in a Scrum way (specifically a Kanban Chart) showing what you have To Do, are Doing, and have Done.

Entry date	Phase	Magnitude	Priority	Category	Item
13-Mar	Doing	BIG	1	Attraction	Descriptor
19-Feb	To Do	Bite	2	Retention	Descriptor
12-Jan	xDone		5	Performance	Descriptor
19-Feb	Doing		2	Clients	Descriptor
20-Feb	To Do		3	Client BID	Descriptor
14-Mar	Doing		1	HR System/Task	Descriptor
13-Mar	Doing	BIG	1	Attraction	Descriptor
19-Feb	To Do	Bite	5	Retention	Descriptor
12-Jan	xDone		2	Performance	Descriptor
19-Feb	Doing - Deleg		WAITING	Clients	Descriptor
20-Feb	To Do		3	Client BID	Descriptor
14-Mar	Doing		4	HR System/Task	Descriptor

Rule # 29 - Doing more with less

I truly hate this expression. You cannot do more with less it's a mathematical impossibility. What you can do is less and then perhaps you can do less with less. So:

- Learn to say no, and mean it.
- OK, learn to say No constructively by stepping through the ask and exploring the obstacles.
    - *I can't get all of this done by Tuesday* – won't work, I've tried it.
    - *I will focus on the following for Tuesday* – and hope they agree, they did. They didn't forget

about the rest but by Tuesday, having made progress, it seemed less essential.

- Communicate efficiently, the classic example is the one-hour meeting, do we always need one hour, sixty contiguous minutes? Could we email material in advance, recap it at the beginning and be out of there in thirty? Did you bring your garrote for the voice that says "since we're here can we discuss blah blah?". Something no-one came prepared to discuss and the only answer is "no" and then the 'be supportive' voice in your head pleads with you to say, "but let's schedule time to do that after you have summarised the issue to us in an email." Plus, winning smile and packing your stuff into your arms/pockets as you stand to leave the room or press the little red phone sign for hang up on the speaker phone.

Charm can be helpful but it can take a lifetime to develop and should not be relied upon. Best to be yourself and always be thinking of the greater good even if it's a lonely outpost.

Rule # 30 - Normalization of Deviance

These are the scariest three words you will ever hear, Normalisation of Deviance.

You know I can hear you when you're sniggering.

What does it mean?

A small adjustment, error if you will, that if tolerated, compounds over time. This is a classic issue in accident, disaster scenarios but is equally applicable in the drift to complication.

Let me help you visualise it:

I always reverse into my garage. I use the back-up camera every time.

I always reverse into my garage. I sometimes use the back-up camera but sometimes I just know how far I am from the door by using the brush hanging on the wall.

I do it every day. I don't need the back-up camera.

I always reverse into my garage but only once did my husband surprise me with the door open and a cake in his hand for my birthday. Luckily, I only killed the cake.

This is an example of Normalisation of Deviance.

Instead work to normalize that which you value and not the deviations from process (unless you want to formally change the process).

Always applaud simplification, no matter how slight, never spit in its eye.

Rule # 31 – Don't Multi-task

The giant learning from computers doing a number of things at the same time is that it is impossible. However, computers are a mystery to most people. Far from learning, we flip between tasks, we call it multi-taking (computers call it context switching). Any delusion you have about being effective across multiple tasks, forget it. In computing they have a word for when it gets really crazy and that's *thrashing* which makes the computer so inefficient it all but gives up. How it is generally avoided in computers is that we throw resources at the problem, rarely done for humans.

What we all do when we multi-task is step out of the task we are in and then ramp up in the new task. Every single time we then expend (waste) time on the ramp-down and then the ramp-up. Interrupt a person several times in an hour and you can risk them achieving nothing at all.

Then, there's the nightmare that is open plan ... a bazillion interruptions, constantly. Sold as a collaboration tool, as Susan Cain writes in her almost perfect treatise on introverts, Quiet, '...top performers overwhelmingly worked for companies that gave their works...privacy, personal space... freedom from interruption.'

We multi-task because we think faster than we speak that doesn't mean we have to let it take control. My dog runs faster than me back to the car but that doesn't mean he gets to drive the car.

How can you simplify your task management?

- Timebox - Set minimum amounts of time to spend on things (computer operating systems like Linux work on things for at least ¾ second – I'd suggest a lot more for humans, like several minutes).
- Lumping – look at all your postal mail say once a day.

Rule # 32 – Understand why people don't do things

The Walter Reed Army Medical Center figured out that a lot of eye injuries were caused because people weren't wearing their safety glasses so they created cooler eyewear, people wore them and they got fewer eye injuries.

Rule # 33 – Attend fewer meetings

You will need to attend meetings from time to time to discuss what you are doing. With Scrum you will need to attend meetings such as the fifteen-minute daily stand-up but these meetings have a strong purpose and a tight timeline.

It is a truism to state that many, many, meetings are boring. The more insecure the person running the meeting the more the tendency to tedium expands. In explaining the need to simplify think like the 12-storey ocean cruise liner, it's only OK until the Tsunami hits, then nothing will save you.

Also realise that people call meetings to reassure themselves, about what I have not yet figured out but from the self-satisfaction on their faces, I often think it's just the power they have to call multiple people into a room and make them sit there against their will.

The other meeting challenge is the late arrival. I knew a PM who solved that quickly by getting the reputation for always locking the door. No-one was late twice.

Check out Lencioni's, Death by Meetings referenced in the Bookshelf.

Rule # 34 – Your personal behaviour

Marshall Goldsmith, a man I have not met, but I have met people who have eaten with him so perhaps that's a form of acquaintance. His list describing the characteristics that will let you down as you progress in your career is a pretty good list of how to fail when you are trying to simplify. The key to simplification is to share and be open but in case that's not enough for you let me be more specific, do NOT:

1. Win too much
2. Add too much value (let other people speak)
3. Pass judgement

4. Make destructive comments
5. Start with NO, BUT or HOWEVER
6. Tell the world how smart you are
7. Speak when angry
8. Be negative (who cares if you already know why it won't work, let them have an idea)
9. Withhold information (and don't smirk like you have a huge secret)
10. Fail to give proper recognition
11. Claim credit you don't deserve
12. Make excuses
13. Cling to the past
14. Play favourites
15. Fail to Listen
16. Fail to express your gratitude
17. Punish the messenger

18. Pass the buck

19. Have an excessive need to be YOU

And if you can't manage to follow this guidance and don't feel remorse or beg for forgiveness if you fail then take this book and throw it in the trash now and remove yourself from interactions with the rest of us.

On a more constructive note, you can also check out Neuro-Linguistic Programming (NLP) and Emotional Intelligence (EQ) referenced in the Bookshelf section. Did you know? You can improve your EQ but not your IQ.

Rule # 35 – Reject conventional wisdom

My favourite sports coach Bill Belichick of the New England Patriots rejects conventional wisdom all the time. He is reluctantly assuming the mantle of Best Coach of ALL time as he attends yet another Superbowl and claims another victory. He's been known to admonish his players who try to do more than they can, in other words make the task more complicated, his oft quoted expression "Just Do Your Job" now adorns T-shirts and can be heard being applied to other teams.

The perfect is the enemy of the good

Voltaire

8. LEADERSHIP

It's probably time to discuss the other elephant in the room (the first being time management and how to eat one). Yes, yes, servant leader, blah blah but it's true. Leaders aren't gods they are obstacle removers. Product Owners remove obstacles to enable the project to run at maximum efficiency. If you want it, you will help!

Leadership is about knowing the people you work with, therefore, it's useful to run regular skip level meetings with those below that first manager barrier. It's also important that when you hear enough issues about a manager, trust me, it's not an over-reaction to eventually fire them. However, don't rush to replace them, try acting in that role for a while and see what happens. Make the freed group of managers, or individual contributors, work as a collective in a functional sense, attending your status meetings.

Never be afraid of your managers' work, up or

down, always be ready to take it over, that way, no one ever has the best of you, in any direction. Green-eyed, and staring at you from their green throne can make power go to any cat's head.

Other tips that have stood me in good stead as a leader and Project Manager are:

- Wear clothes with proper pockets (for pens, notepaper, phones…)
- Dress to command respect, work is not the prom, so don't make the pockets clown like
- Assume you are dispensable and be professional enough to file and keep up to date project folders
- Keep a decision log however rudimentary (Decision, who, when)
- Always carry a pen and a note pad (yellow stickie notes, two inches by two inches is ample) or have a notepad you understand and can operate on your mobile/cell phone.

Rule # 36 – Team performance is everything

Make every work waking moment be the time when you think about how to make it easier, simpler. This will eventually lead to greater speed and what in Scrum terms is known as Velocity. Velocity is the increase in speed at which you achieve progress in Sprints and you get closer to your goal. Teams grow in confidence and capability, supported as they are, and enabled to focus.

If you are a leader, people will block your progress, some spectacularly, others subtly.

If you are an individual, people will block your progress, some spectacularly, others subtly.

Do they want it to be better, or don't they?

Those who block must be confronted and the nature of their blockage removed.

- When you...

- I feel...

- How does that make you feel?

- What can we do to improve...?

Rule # 37 – Understand complexity

Complexity piles up around us like regret. Previously simple things aggregate to create the complex, and this can be good, like Lego building bricks; you can take simple bricks and build a castle. Or bad complexity, like individual forms for each special purpose to come together as a giant administrative nightmare, like the Spanish house buying system in the twentieth century, and perhaps still. In searching for the simple to build the complex, or, a better word, the sophisticated, you need to find your minimum set of Lego bricks. As the creator of the Linux operating system, Linus Torvald, said, "An ugly system is one in which there are special interfaces for everything you want to do". Imagine a car with three seats for families of three, another for families with two dogs and four children, one dog and five children, the permutations in the millions, the car sales staff, a plague on the planet (the bad ones). He goes on to compare the beauty (simplicity) of the English alphabet of twenty six characters against Egyptian hieroglyphs where you need a picture for each word (complex) ... not that dissimilar to Chinese, a language so complex that children have to spend extra time at school to learn all the characters. When looking at your problem, what are your twenty six characters?

Torvald also explains that it isn't just about mandating that everything be simple because then the interactions between the simple items become complex. It's like allowing yourself to only use one hundred words and having to say things like, 'I find that I cannot live without your care and affection' all for the sake of one special word, loaded with meaning and allowing you to say, 'I love you' instead.

There are a number of ways to make something complex and they fall into the following buckets:

1. Over consult
2. Too much documentation
3. Employ a consultant to design it
4. Fail to look back and learn

But the real problem is Fear. Fear of upsetting someone. Fear of doing something the boss doesn't like.

The more important whatever it is, is to you, or your boss, the less likely you are to let it go. But if you don't change you will become extinct. When is your idea getting old? Check in on it from time to time. Ask yourself, what would you do if you weren't afraid?

Shine the light.

Rule # 38 - Don't try and keep up

Tic Tac Toe – an unwinnable game. As we race to add more and more (systems, products, offerings) to appear to keep up with others then we enter an unwinnable game.

The Phone business is like this and as we approach 2020, one wonders when it will burn itself out, if it hasn't already.

Rule # 39 – Fail Fast

Linus Torvald, of Linux Operating Systems (computer genius) fame has opinions when it comes to leadership, "instead of trying to hide (from problems) ... the leader must be able to convince everybody that the best thing to do is to go back and start over, which means breaking stuff... (and because of office politics) they need to be someone with a strong personality."

One of the significant improvements that the Scrum approach delivers is the constant pressure to demonstrate progress. This enables failures to be identified early and adjustments to be made. It can be uncomfortable to create something that at the Sprint Review, the invited team and Product Owner, rejects but it is better to know that after two weeks than after two years. How many billions of dollars have been wasted on projects that never see the light of day because either no-one wants them anymore or they are entirely the wrong answer to the original request?

Fail fast!

Rule # 40 – Appreciate the complexity of the Superbowl numbering system and wave it goodbye

Few people can translate roman numerals without some effort. Imagine trying to do long division and multiplication with them (and don't cheat by thinking in our decimal system). Superbowl 50, discreetly dropped the L, because Superbowl L looked odd. The 99th Superbowl will be XCIX at which point people will stop even trying to figure out what it means unless they study Latin. Unless of course the whole Superbowl is really not anything about football and just a way to get us all to move back to the Roman Empire.

Rule # 41 – Learn from Google

In 2012, Google stumbled on what has been known for centuries but web designers are just discovering, "visually complex websites are … less beautiful than their simpler counterparts." I was tempted to write the word Duh here but they are a multi-billion dollar company and it's reassuring they finally figured it out. Duh would also be somewhat against the Scrum ethos. Duh!

Rule # 42 - Fight the perk war

If someone decides to come work for you because you have an indoor Jacuzzi then they maybe shouldn't be your first hiring choice.

Look for people who can help, not hinder.

Remember, the only reason we have companies is because the sum of the parts is greater than the whole enabling us to get more stuff done together. When we confuse it by making it complex, especially in Silicon Valley, people break off and create leaner, nimbler organisations. If this starts to happen to your company then there should be a giant alarm bell going off in your head as you are about to go extinct.

Nature is pleased with simplicity. And nature is no dummy.

Isaac Newton

9. TOOLS YOU CAN USE

So far, this book probably felt like a smattering of Scrum, where's the meat? True that. If you really want to dig into all the detail of Scrum and you don't want to just go for it using Chapter 3 or the one page guide in the Appendix (a real one this time not like the possibly non-existent one of how to kill your boss) then have at it.

However, if you want to continue with tools to support you in your quest to succeed with Scrum, and even its originator has failed in some organisations (to their detriment it must be said), then please press on.

Rule # 43 – Learn to Sort

For obsessive maniacs, the idea that you can NOT efficiently sort everything will come as a shock. The key to administrative sorting (as opposed to how computers do it) is the robustness of the method which means it needs to be easy and it needs to be repeatable.

Computers teach us that keeping around pieces of information you refer to frequently is a smart thing to do. They call it caching and we call it files or paper.

Sorting and prioritizing skills are needed when you are preparing your work, your Product Backlog.

Rule # 44 – Be selective

Being selective is good too, my husband can recall far too much, but I forget plenty. Sherlock Holmes tells us that as you add knowledge, eventually it muscles out other memories so it's important to remember the useful stuff, like our wedding anniversary – just as a very unimportant example that apparently my puny memory can recall but others, cannot.

Rule # 45 – Exploit geography

Exploit geography and have things close to where they are used and know where they will be when you need them again later. A stapler next to the photocopier is useful (let's not delude ourselves that in small companies anyone, and I mean anyone, fills up the automated stapler in the printer – or even knows how to order them or where the manual is located). Your Product Backlog, printed and in your notebook, is useful, and handy. This can also be achieved with a lightweight computer (even a phone) but be sure it will work for you and isn't just to impress people.

Rule # 46 – Don't alphabetize your personal files

Filing rooms seem like an anachronism but they can be swift and efficient ways to find data but even if you don't have a file room you probably have files that you use.

You may try to alphabetize your personal files, don't. Instead have them rest in whatever order you find them and as you use them put the file to the left-most side of the filing area. If you then search from the left, in time you will find that the files you use have gravitated to the left. You may find that those to the right are really not important at all and can be shredded, more permanently filed, or scanned into the computer.

This guidance only works for your desks; thousands of employee files still need to be filed alphabetically and ideally electronically. However, if you pay attention when you next use your computer you may notice the idea of recently used files, it's really not that different.

Rule # 47 – Tabulate

Item	Starting position	Simplified / Cost management idea	Final state	Status
Use of checklists	Rely on knowledge and memory. Undocumented processes.			Not started
Learning from mistakes	Post-mortems. Learnings seldom applied.	Pre-mortem – think about what could go wrong and plan for it.		Work In Progress (WIP)
Voluntary terminations	Personalised letter explaining what happens to their particular benefits	Publish standard policy that answers all questions, evolve it where it doesn't. Send the employee to look for it.	Self-service of required items	Complete
Involuntary termination calculations	Personalised based on standard formula. Open to apparent negotiation	Publish the formula. Refer all queries to legal.		WIP

Rule # 48 – Decision making shortcuts

When making decisions, consider, being satisfied with:

- Less information
- Less computation
- Less time

More really is less when it comes to certain decisions. You need to decide when perfect is too much.

Here's when to think a little less and avoid analysis paralysis:

- When expectations are uncertain

- When the data is noisy (confused or confusing)
- When broad brush, big brush, is really the goal

Dropping the ball such as missing an email can seem like a bad thing. However, we now live in company cultures where they really expect you to have read every email. Madness. The only remedy here is speed reading or parsing your email. You need to latch on to certain names and hope you have picked wisely.

Rule # 49 – Less choice is faster

Give people fewer choices and they choose faster and with more certainty. Successful parents apply this rule every day, they can even turn it into a closed decision but take care:

Red or blue socks?

(closed, limited choice)

No socks.

(children can confound us)

Better:

It is very cold today, so you can play outside you need to wear socks. Red or blue?

Red.

Besides the noble art of getting things done, there is the noble art of leaving things undone. The wisdom of life consists in the elimination of non-essentials.

Lin Yutang

10. CHANGING

There are always trends in Management Science and one recent one has been something called VUCA. Bennett and Lemoine have a snappy guide to VUCA that was published in the Harvard Business Review in 2014.

VUCA originated in the US Military as a way to step back and think about a situation.

First off what does VUCA mean:

V = Volatility

U = Uncertainty

C = Complexity

A = Ambiguity

In a Scrum context, this could look like:

Volatility	Be prepared	
Uncertainty	Research	Keep checking and adjusting the Product Backlog
Complexity	Simplify	
Ambiguity	Fail fast	Sprints

Rule # 50 - Expect change resistance

Direct resistance is easy to spot. Employees pick machines off the wall with their fork-lift truck and run over them, by accident! The indirect kind is subtler. Things you might see are:

- More and more detail requested, endless questions
- Not able to find a time to implement
- Debating definitions and concepts
- Pressing for solutions too soon
- Blame someone else for lack of progress
- Expressing a gut feeling that something is wrong
- Unclear where they stand

Reach into them and pull the issue out and slap it on the table and discuss it into being direct resistance or a resolved issue. This might be a group activity or one on one. You decide!

Rule # 51 – Go to the Heath

The Heath brothers say it best so borrowing from their book as a way to SWITCH someone's behaviour with a worked example of a Scrum project to simplify sign-offs in HR:

DIRECT	Follow the bright spot	Payroll have started sending out forms in template emails, to great success.
	Script the critical moves	Cite the Payroll example to others and explain how to set up a template email.
	Point to the destination	Give examples of ways the template emails could be used for your group.
MOTIVATE	Find the feeling	Talk about how painful it can be to get signatures from that VP on the 9th floor.
	Shrink the change	Suggest they try just one, nothing too important, see how it goes.
	Grow your people	Point them at the problem, don't micromanage them through this. Think parent at the school gate.
SHAPE	Tweak the environment	Socialise the idea of template emails as being modern and trendy.
	Build habits	Ask a question every time you get the chance. Could this form be a template email?
	Rally the herd	Make an example for another team. Help the idea proliferate.

Then think about the tasks you want to work on and prioritize them:

> Critical now – real time savers, something you do all the time – TODAY
>
> Opportunity for future savings – next ten days
>
> Over the horizon – future.

Rule # 52 – Tiny changes

To help doctors provide neater hand-written instructions some researchers have shared powerful, but simple, images as to the effect of their sloppy handwriting on the death or near-death experiences of patients because of their hand-writing having been mis-read by say a pharmacist.

(The Heath brothers have a lot of powerful examples in their Switch book).

Rule # 53 – Thinking negatively is a good thing

What could go wrong?

Don't over do it but thinking about the daft things others could do, trawling your memory for things someone might have forgotten, you might have forgotten, stuff that happened before.

Red Team techniques are leaking out of the military and into the commercial space as a vehicle to harness critical thinking, identifying potential issues or mis-interpretations. This technique celebrates the idea we know as Devil's

Advocate. Check out the Bookshelf for more details.

Rule # 54 – Think small

Often, we want to boil the ocean when really it's just a cup of tea that is needed.

The simple step of slowing down can reduce errors and therefore reduce the impact of repeat work.

For example:

Proof read.

"Could you read over this for me?" should be a mandatory question for anyone producing a piece of work to be read or used by another human.

Rule # 55 – Automate

Stare hard at a situation and see what tools the company is using that can be better applied or that can be used to help.

Simple example:

These days we all want to know what kinds of people work for companies: green, orange, whatever. The easiest way is to collect it when they are hired. The stupid thing is to then just file that form. Pull a few facts from it and shove it in a useful field in your Payroll system and then if the employee wishes to change from orange to green, they can choose themselves and you are just running an anonymous report.

When someone wants to know how many green people we employ then, no angst.

Rule # 56 – Effectuate...

Effectuate – bring to pass.

No decision needed.

Simple example:

If we don't hear from you by the last day of your third month of hire, you will automatically be enrolled in the pension scheme with a deduction of 5% from your salary that will matched by 5% from the company. This amount will be placed in the Fixed Income account.

This wording has extra benefits, we don't have to look up and specify the exact date the employee was hired since we are using a distance in time from their start date which they knew. Less work for us in looking it up. One fewer decision for the employee in those critical first ninety days. When our task pops up for action we do it or better yet we have it programmed so that it automatically happens if we don't make any changes. This last approach has the added benefit that if we forget, something will happen.

The only thing necessary for the triumph of evil is for good men to do nothing.

Edmund Burke

(Irish c. 1740 – not sure why you need this extra detail but old wisdom is so there, don't you think? Well, if you put the whole inquisition, persecution of innocents stuff aside.)

And

The true measure of a man is how he treats someone who can do him absolutely no good.

Samuel Johnson

(also old – 1709 - 84)

11. YOU

A line I heard recently that has stuck with me:

(we) Judge ourselves by our intentions but judge others by their behaviour.

Stephen Covey, 2006

Doesn't that just smack you in the head? We meant well, but, them, they are evil.

Rule # 57 -
Ritualize your day

At 7am I take 15 mins and see what needs to be done for the day. I create my priority list.

At 7.30am I check email and adjust my priority list for the day (which can involve wholesale changes but at least I know who I plan to disappoint today).

At 8.30am I hold my daily Sprint Stand-up.

Once every hour I take a minute or so to look over my list and refocus

At 9.45am I take 5 mins and do nothing.

At 11.55am I take 5 mins and do nothing.

At the end of the day, before I leave, I see what was achieved and what we or I will be coming back to in the morning by studying the Sprint Board showing: To Do, Doing, Done.

Some days it's the end of the Sprint. It almost feels like a form of therapy to look back. I want to know how to improve (and not who to blame):

- What went right?

- What could have gone better?

- What can be better in the next Sprint?

By the end of the discussion myself, the Scrum Master, and the team agree on the one process improvement we can commit to for the next Sprint and action it immediately as we plan the next Sprint.

Rule # 58 – Filter out the unessential

The Duke of Wellington was famous for remaining calm at the Battle of Waterloo. Despite the turmoil he filtered out what was unthreatening (even if noisy) and concentrated on what was essential. He won, beating Napoleon (there's a guy who would have benefited from end of project reflection).

It would not shock me to learn that Bill Belichick (coach for the NFL's New England Patriots) and the Duke were related.

Rule # 59 – Be trusted

Customers and clients are happy to be led. You are the expert you tell them what to do. You, as the expert, took the time to pick things for them and they will go with your choice. I don't tell Fortnum and Mason what to put in their standard hampers. I trust them and they send them on my behalf. We're all happy, so long as I don't get the Piccalilli (a form of sickly torture in a sickly sauce – I may be biased).

Conflict is inevitable and when it happens, remember:

- Healthy, natural expression of our feeling is OK.

- Centre yourself and always get back to emotionally neutral

- Re-direct the energy of the discussion onto something to move the problem forward.

- Clarify any statements to get to the facts, not to the feelings.

It's important to avoid the volcano of unmet needs that people carry around like luggage. Realise that trust takes time to build and, most important of all, listen to understand, not defend!

Rule # 60 – Speed but not at any cost

Speed can help – faster decisions, fewer choices, remove time, remove access. In the rush for speed we can unintentionally run over passers by.

BUT never forget:

Whether your boss, their boss, or your direct reports, or theirs, always speak to people as if they are your equal. Be seen to be fair and not just say you are fair.

It's not that different with kids. You see people who talk to babies and young children in some weird made up language like they are morons. Use simpler language but don't treat them like simpletons, the same applies to colleagues.

Never throw your weight around, when you need to do that then you have the problem, not them.

Rule # 61 - Take 5 minute breaks

And do exactly nothing. It's good for you

and you will be more productive.

Tragically, a policeman was killed by a driver who was asleep at the wheel. This is played out across the planet daily…

Take a break.

Rule # 62 - Make Simplicity and Scrum part of your brand

Why not? We notice happy people why not productive people?

Incidentally, happy people are often more creative problem solvers. They also make decisions more quickly, with less hesitation and post-decisional regret.

From this I conclude, be a happy ambassador of Simplification and Scrum.

Rule # 63 – Managing expectations when you have more than one project

When you have a project, it is hard to keep everyone happy. When you have more than one project it's impossible. Unless you are putting out a lot of fires or have the hysterical type of boss alluded to in these pages then here's a way to balance happiness:

2 projects – both due this week.

Project 1: Estimated project duration = 1 day. Start this one immediately and deliver it early.

Project 2: Estimated project duration = 4 day. Start this one tomorrow and deliver it later than was requested on Friday but explain that will be the case on Tuesday.

This is not a panacea but hopefully you get the idea. Communicate constantly. Work on your apology speech and use it regularly until it becomes second nature. Who cares if it's not your fault, the objective is unrelenting delivery.

Rule # 64 - Don't take the monkey

We all do it. Someone talks about a problem and we end up taking it. It can be as simple as someone saying, "We've got a problem with …" A problem that until that moment you didn't know you had and you

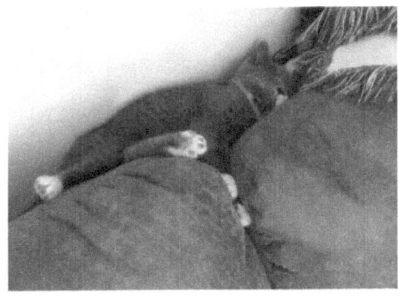

say "Let me think about it." They toddle off unburdened, relaxing completely and now you have the problem. The monkey is now on your back and they're passed out on the back of the sofa.

Rule # 65 – Completed Staff Work

If you lead a team in any way, shape or form, you need to follow the doctrine of Completed Staff Work.

What you may be wondering, is that? It's an approach taught in the military. The essence of it is:

- Don't let people come with problems and barf them onto your desk, like a furball (it's a cat thing).

- Get them to come with a problem plus thought out recommendations.

- Better yet, have team members who take actions from you and update you through your normal processes.

Managers run out of time. Subordinates run out of work.

Rule # 66 – Don't be 'that' boss

Many business books talk about how telling the boss bad news reduces your chances of upward mobility – I do not believe this to be untrue. Yep, you read me right, but I wrote it in a convoluted or complicated way to see if you were still with me. In other words, it's TRUE (mostly) that bad news to the Boss can be career limiting. However, rising to the top, dying prematurely, missing your kid's school play, missing out on one of life's real joys, having children in the first place (correct, I am still not a grandmother and this is a shameless guilt trip for a certain someone) isn't as much fun as it sounds.

Money fixes nothing. Mundane work, or work that might fall under the descriptor 'cruel and unusual punishment', will be done for money only until there is a better option.

Rule # 67 – Know your part in the process

Maryann Keller in her book Rude Awakening talks about a car worker who didn't know what a part they fitted did and so was unaware that if it was even slightly wrong a big piece had to be ripped out – the carpet – to fix it.

Daniel Gilbert's experiments on the Harvard Campus showed that having more choice reduced happiness and caused decision fatigue.

Every day we make a bazillion decisions. Why? Can we have fewer?

Blue Apron currently offers meal preparation in a box, to your door. Meat counters in supermarkets offer chopped chicken breast with the sauce alongside it. Romaine lettuce is chopped for us and bagged with the Caesar salad dressing alongside it. I'm not saying these are good things but in a world with too many decisions something has to give to reduce the volume.

Personally, I can spend weeks at a time when I am insanely busy basically wearing the same collection of trousers, socks and shirts (fresh ones each day before you ask, laundered at the weekend to start the whole sorry saga again the next week). By simplifying my clothing decisions, I have more time for important decisions or even just other decisions.

Rule # 68 - Hire independent thinkers then expect blind obedience

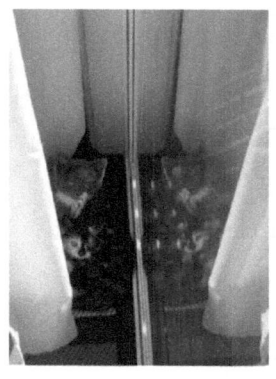

It's true that we hire people hoping for their creative input until they creatively input in a way we don't like. Resist the temptation to slap them down. Be the bigger person. Listen.

Rule # 69 - Simplifying is an easy rope to loosen

Surrounded as we can be by control freaks, the easiest thing for anyone to personally do is to make their job simpler or work with like minded individuals to change something together. Even if the boss's boss is a raving lunatic, even then, some simple can slide through. It can be dressed up as more 'other work', but it let's folk leave on time, more refreshed, able to create and make fewer mistakes. This is what I mean about simplification being about you, as much as anyone.

Rule # 70 – Work expands to fill the available time

Parkinson's Law, "work expands so as to fill the time available for its completion".

Who hasn't seen this in action?

Do NOT do this. STOP now!

...it's really more intelligent to be able to simplify things than to complicate them. Even if some people think it makes you look stupid.

Eugenia Cheng

Appendix – Scrum Short Guide

Monitoring and actioning project work by applying Scrum techniques

You eat an elephant, one bite at a time.

Your Project's Requirement List = Product Backlog

Step 1:

Take the project's requirements list:

a. Create a list of all the work that needs to be done and split it into chunks.
b. Each chunk needs to have a tangible deliverable (e.g. a list of data, a working screen, a user handout, a form, a set of interviews).
c. For each chunk, who needs to help?

d. Is that chunk of work: Small (few hours), Medium (maybe a day) or Large (a few days – and if so, can it be split into smaller chunks?)?
e. Sort the list into priority order with the most important items at the top. You will need to consider chunks that are needed first before another chunk can be worked on, for example, interview questions prepared *before* the interviews. You now have your Product Backlog.

Step 2:

a. What can be done by the next meeting (the Sprint Review)?

Step 3:

Using a whiteboard, noticeboard, spare piece of wall, any large surface devoid of artwork, create your own tracking system with sticky notes of all the chunks of project work you are doing for this Sprint. Start them all in the To Do column and move them over as you complete them:

All the project chunks	To Do for this Sprint	Doing	Done
...	...	...	...

This is known as a Kanban board.

Step 4:

Meet every single business day for a Stand-up (as in standing only) for no more than 15 minutes ideally at a set time each day. Each person answers the following questions:

a. What was done yesterday to finish the Sprint?
b. What will be done today?
c. What are the obstacles to achieving the goal?

Step 5:

The Sprint Review becomes:

a. What was accomplished since the last Review with an actual artefact like a process or a job description or something you can proudly show people.
b. Is that item completely ready to go, no more work (on that chunk not the total project)?

At the meeting you then ask – in a blame-free way:

a. What went right?
b. What could have been better? What would make you happier?
c. What one improvement can we make to help work be better in the next Sprint?

Rinse and repeat until done.

Appendix – How to Estimate

What follows is a very quick guide to an easy to visualise estimating tool that is intended to lure you into making tricky decisions by obscuring the detail.

1. Develop a task list of what you want.
2. Prioritise it using some type of metric. Classics are: Urgent, High, Low, Nice to have.
3. Estimate the level of effort to complete each task. Borrowing from the Scrum book noted in the Bookshelf use

something familiar like the following to estimate the task size:

    a. Goldfish – a day or less
    b. Kitten – 1 to 3 days
    c. Labradoodle – 4 to 7 days
    d. Horse – 7 to 10 days
    e. Elephant – need to be broken down into smaller chunks

4. Look at each task and discuss as a group which of Goldfish to Elephant it is. If it's an Elephant then you need to break it down into smaller animals.

You now have a prioritised and estimated Product Backlog that you need to choose from with your Product Owner to create the To Do list for your first Sprint.

BOOKSHELF

Bennett N. and Lemoine G.J. What VUCA really means for you. Harvard Business Review. January-February 2014 issue.

Black, Octavius and Bailey, Sebastien. The Mindgym. 2005. Time Warner Books, London, UK.

Boyes, Carolyn. NLP (Neuro-Linguistic Programming). 2006. Collins, London, UK.

Cain, Susan. Quiet. 2013. Random House, New York, NY, USA.

Christian, Brian and Griffiths. Tom Algorithms to live by – the computer science of human decisions. 2016, Allen Lane hardcover by Penguin Canada.

Daniel Gilbert's experiments on the Harvard Campus.

Fortnum and Masons, www.fortnumandmason.com. Since 1707.

Frankl, Viktor, E.. Man's Search for Meaning. 2006. Beacon Press, Boston, MA, USA.

Goldsmith, Marshall. What got you here won't get you there. 2007. Hyperion, New York, NY, USA.

Heath, Chip and Dan, Switch – How to change things when change is hard. 2010. Random House, New York, NY, USA.

Hiatt, Jeffery M. . Employee's Survival Guide to Change. 2004. Prosci Research, Learning Center Publications.

Hobbs, Peter. DK Essential Managers – Project Management. 2009. Dorling Kindersley Limited, London, UK.

Hoffman, Bryce G.. Red Teaming. 2017. Crown Publishing, New York, NY, USA.

Idaho Public Television or whatever Public station television is near you.

IIL International - IPM Day 2018 (and any of their International Project Management days)

Keller, Maryann. Rude Awakening. 1989. William Morrow and Co., USA.

Kluger, Jeffrey. Simplexity. 2008. Hyperion, New York, NY, USA.

Kondo, Marie. The life-changing magic of tidying up – the Japanese art of decluttering and organizing. 2014. Ten Speed Press part of Penguin Random House Company, New York, NY, USA.

Larson, Diana and Nies, Ainsley. 2006. The Pragmatic Programmers, LLC.

Lencioni, Patrick. Death by Meeting. 2004. Wiley, SF, CA, USA.

Lyengar, Sheena. The Art of Choosing. 2010. Twelve, Hatchett Book Group, New York, NY, USA.

Regents of the University of California, 2002. The Whitehall Studies. Interview with Professor Marmot - http://globetrotter.berkeley.edu/people2/Marmot/marmot-con3.html accessed June 4, 2016.

Sapolsky, Robert M., Why Zebras don't get ulcers. 2004. Henry Holt and Company, New York, NY, USA.

Stein, Steven J, and Book, Howard E.. The EQ Edge, Emotional intelligence and your success. 2006. John Wiley, Mississauga, ON, Canada.

Sutherland, Jeff and J.J. – Scrum The art of doing Twice the work in half the time. Crown Publishing, New York, NY, USA.

Torvalds, Linus and Diamond, David. Just for Fun – the story of an accidental revolutionary. 1999 ZDNet published by HarperCollins, New York, NY, USA.

Tufte, Edward R. – all his books but if I had to choose, The Visual Display of Quantitative Information. 2001. Graphics Press, Cheshire, CT, USA.

Ward, Dan. The Simplicity Cycle. 2015. Harper Collins, New York, NY, USA.

Weller, Jac. On Wellington. The Duke and his Art of War. 1998. Greenhill Books, London, UK.

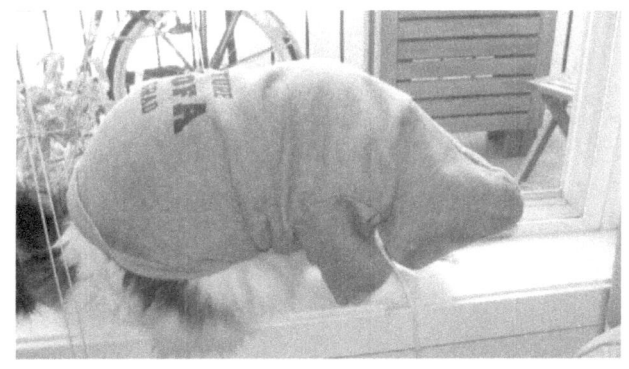

Her next move was to wriggle out backwards, push pass the photographer, jump down, pause, and clean her paw.

Susan Anthony - originally from the heart of the British Isles, arriving in Alberta, Canada via Massachusetts, USA. A lover of big cats and small adventures, or is it the other way around? Susan has worked in technology, non-profit, leisure, rescue services etc..

Her motto is, 'Eat when you can. Pee when you can.' that she borrowed from a Tom Clancy character.